Machine Learning For Beginners

An Introduction for Beginners, Why Machine Learning Matters Today and How Machine Learning Networks, Algorithms, Concepts and Neural Networks Really Work

Steven Cooper

Legal & Disclaimer

The following document is reproduced below with the goal of providing information that is as accurate and reliable as possible.

This declaration is deemed fair and valid by both the American Bar Association and the Committee of Publishers Association and is legally binding throughout the United States.

Furthermore, the transmission, duplication or reproduction of any of the following work including specific information will be considered an illegal act irrespective of if it is done electronically or in print. This extends to

Table of Contents

Preface ix

Introduction 1

Chapter 1: Machine Learning - What and Why? 7

Chapter 2: Machine Learning vs. Artificial Intelligence and Deep Learning 13

Reflection Questions 20

Chapter 3: Machine Learning Workflows 21

Reflection Questions 28

Chapter 4: About Computer Learning (Supervised, Unsupervised, Reinforcement) 29

Reflection Questions 45

Chapter 5: Supervised Learning 47

Parametric/Non-Parametric Algorithms 51

Linear Regression 54

Parametric Problems 58

Logistic Regression 62

Non-Parametric Algorithms - K-Nearest Neighbors 63

Decision Trees 71

Support Vector Machines 74

Kernels 77

Reflection Questions 78

Chapter 6: Unsupervised Learning 79

Clustering 81

Dimensionality Reduction 84

Neural Networks 85

Deep Learning 95

Reflection Questions 101

Chapter 7: Reinforcement Learning ...103

Reflection Questions 109

Chapter 8: Best Practices in Machine Learning **111**

Focus on One Discipline at a Time 112

Don't Reinvent the Wheel 116

Work with Other Projects 118

Reflection Questions 120

Chapter 9: Learning Algorithms and Applications **121**

Learning Algorithms 122

Text-based Services 123

Computer Vision 127

Audio Processing 129

Database Mining 132

Reflection Questions 133

Chapter 10: Examples of Successful Machine Learning **135**

Spotify and Pandora 136

PayPal 138

Uber....140

Facebook....141

Gmail....145

Closing....147

Reflection Questions....148

Chapter 11: Future of Machine Learning....149

Finance....150

Language....152

Medical Industry....153

Self-Driving Cars....154

Robots and Androids....156

Closing....158

Reflection Questions....159

Conclusion....161

About the Author....167

Preface

The main goal of this book is to help people take the best actionable steps possible towards a career in data science. The need for data scientists is growing exponentially as the internet, and online services continue to expand.

Book Objectives

This book will help you:

- ✓ Know more about the fundamental principles of data science and what you need to become a skilled data scientist.
- ✓ Have an elementary grasp of data science concepts and tools that will make this work easier to do.
- ✓ Have achieved a technical background in data science and appreciate its power.

Target Users

The book is designed for a variety of target audiences. The most suitable users would include:

- Newbies in computer science techniques
- Professionals in software applications development and social sciences
- Professors, lecturers or tutors who are looking to find better ways to explain the content to their students in the simplest and easiest way
- Students and academicians, especially those focusing on data science and software development

Is this book for me?

This book is for those who are interested in data science. There are a lot of skills that a data scientist needs, such as coding, intellectual mindset, eagerness to make new discoveries, and much more.

It’s important that you are interested in this because you are obsessed with this kind of work. Your driving force should not be money. If it is, then this book is not for you.

Introduction

There is absolutely no question about it: artificial intelligence is the future. However, artificial intelligence is also the present. It's one of the faster-growing tech fields and, as I'm sure you're aware, the future is only going to see more and more demand for capable artificial intelligence programmers.

I'm not certain why you're listening to this book. Perhaps you're already on the path to studying artificial intelligence and machine learning in college or a university, and you're wanting a book that will put you on an excellent path forward and help you figure out the context and rationale behind your lessons as you push on. Perhaps you're wanting to switch fields and take advantage of the massive wave of demand that's hitting for artificial intelligence, data analysis, and machine learning as we speak. Or perhaps you're just a hobbyist interested in learning exactly what this machine learning that everybody's talking about is.

Regardless of your ultimate machine, you're reading the right book. This book is intended to break down machine learning and the many, many concepts which build it up.

The book will begin by looking at machine learning and what it is, as well as why one would benefit from looking into machine learning and learning the nuances of this specific area of artificial intelligence. This will give you a clear sense of purpose as you go through the rest of the book and start thinking of ways to apply this in a day-to-day sense.

Afterward, it's going to start breaking the concept of machine learning down into bite-sized chunks. We're going to start with the biggest and most nebulous concepts, and then slowly work our way down to things at the smallest and most intricate levels. We'll be studying the numerous different paradigms for machine learning and how they can be programmed and implemented within your own code, as well as getting a feel for the algorithms which build them up. Throughout all of this, the goal is simply to foster an appreciation for the immense and difficult topic that is machine learning.

The goal at this point is to build a very intimate knowledge of the inner workings of machine learning so that by the time you're finished with all the finer details and the algorithms, you'll be able to go into a deeper level on any of the topics in this book and start to have an idea of how they all work at a more strenuous and taxing level. As such, we're going to be spending a lot of time at the algorithmic level and breaking every type of machine learning down into its various disciplines, as well as discussing the primary terms used within the context of machine learning and what they mean.

After all of that, we're going to start looking at the *applications* of machine learning. This will help you to get a much better feel for machine learning and how it works, which can be a great boon for your understanding of how these many concepts that we're covering can be reasonably applied. This will run the gamut from discussions of anti-spam measures implemented by email providers, to the use of machine learning algorithms in applications like the development of smarter robotics.

This book is being written for the simple reason that I am passionate about machine learning and artificial intelligence. I want to help you to spur your own passion and build a genuine love for these extremely interesting topics. That's why this book is designed with the reader in mind, such that by the end of this book, you feel like your money was well spent. It's not enough for me that you understand the raw concepts - I want you to understand the logic behind everything and understand the reasons behind why certain things are being done the way they are. When you finish this book, I don't want you to feel like you just read it only to read it; I want you to feel as if you gained some valuable insight into machine learning that you wouldn't have been able to get otherwise. I also want you to feel like you are proficient enough with the concepts in your own code.

Moreover, every chapter will end with a few review questions that are intended to give you a solid point to reflect on everything that you've just read and really start to think about the content of the book instead of just passively experiencing it and moving from chapter to chapter. These breaks are meant to gauge your understanding of the content, to flex your brain muscles, and to let you know when you need to go back and revise a concept.

All in all, a lot of work has gone into making a book that will help people to understand this topic that I care so much about. I genuinely hope that it's able to help you in understanding this incredible science. Without further ado, let's go ahead and jump in!

Chapter 1: Machine Learning - What and Why?

"I often tell my students not to be misled by the name 'artificial intelligence' - there is nothing artificial about it. AI is made by humans, intended to behave by humans, and, ultimately, to impact humans' lives and human society."— ***Fei-Fei Li***

Our long and arduous journey begins in this chapter. Over the course of the next several chapters, we're going to be discussing the massively popular and impactful discipline of machine learning. By the end of this book, you're going to have a firm grasp on the underlying concepts that have to do with machine learning.

So, with all of that said - where to begin? I suppose that the easiest place to begin is a discussion of what machine learning is and why it's useful. Bear in mind that this book is going to assume that the reader has a basic knowledge of programming sufficient enough to carry them throughout; some terms will be explained, while others will not.

Artificial intelligence has long lived within the dreamscape of science fiction nuts the world over. For over a century, people have been dreaming of highly sophisticated robots that would do all our bidding and, some think, know us better than we know ourselves.

How much of this is dream and how much of this is reality? That much is hard to say. The discipline is still in its infancy, and there's quite a bit left to learn about the limits of computers and machine-based knowledge. Some posit that we'll be able to create what could essentially be seen as digital "minds." Others who are less optimistic still posit that artificial intelligence is going to have a profound and difficult-to-imagine impact on life as we know it.

Either way, by deciding to understand machine learning and artificial intelligence, you've already taken an important first step towards having a strong understanding of the extremely powerful discipline. So, with all of that said, what is machine learning?

Machine learning, in and of itself, is a relatively simple concept. The idea of machine learning is that computers can actively learn things without somebody programming them specifically to be good at those things. In other words, machine learning is the process of teaching machines to better themselves at any given activity by giving them the tools to algorithmically improve and adjust what they see as "right" and "wrong" in terms of the activity. This allows them to ultimately improve their ability to seek the best and most impacting paths through it.

Many different methods build up machine learning, and machine learning has come to be extremely useful and profoundly impacting, even in its relatively short lifespan. Over the course of this book, we're going to explore numerous different methodologies to machine learning.

Machine learning is built up of two core disciplines: supervised and unsupervised learning. There is also reinforcement learning. Supervised and unsupervised learning in and of themselves are simple to understand and fundamentally different. Regarding them, we will be going in-depth, as well as the techniques which build them up, later in the book. However, for right now, the core difference to note between them is that supervised and unsupervised learning both offer a means by which computers can improve at their ability to *predict data*. One uses some sort of interactive component, *supervised learning*, where unsupervised learning depends on the machine verifying its own techniques and learning/adjusting based off incorrect and correct methods that are discovered in the process.

There are already a huge number of different uses for machine learning out there that have been explored. Among these are uses within the field of data science, where machine learning has been used to develop systems that can be used for predicting future trends based off of the given data, as well as within the fields of medicine, robotic vision, the development of advanced network security systems, and the development of common ameliorations to everyday applications. For instance, advanced spam filters for emails based off of machine learning and Bayesian recognition models.

As this book drives on, you are going to discover more and more numerous different ways in which these methodologies can be applied, as well as better understand the applications themselves. By the time we reach the end, the hope is that you will have a firm enough grasp on the broad and intoxicatingly interesting world of machine learning, such that you can start writing your own applications which work with these concepts.

Chapter 2: Machine Learning vs. Artificial Intelligence and Deep Learning

"I believe this artificial intelligence is going to be our partner. If we misuse it, it will be a risk. If we use it right, it can be our partner." – ***Masayoshi Son***

In this chapter, we're going to dive even further into the idea of machine learning by differentiating it from related disciplines. Namely, machine learning is a pretty major thing right now; a lot of people are learning that it's the next big thing in computing and, as a result, they're trying to jump on the machine learning train by retaining everything they can about machine learning and its related disciplines.

This is great in and of itself, but at the same time, it can kind of muddy the market; people who are getting into machine learning right now are almost certainly familiar with two other concepts: artificial intelligence and deep learning. However, since this book is about machine learning and all these concepts are related but not the same, it's important that we spend some time marking the differences between machine learning and these other disciplines.

First, what is the difference between machine learning and artificial intelligence? This question is extremely simple to answer. Machine learning is to artificial intelligence, as calculus is to mathematics. Therefore, not all artificial intelligence has to do with machine learning, but all of machine learning has to do with artificial intelligence; much like not all of mathematics is calculus, but all of calculus is most certainly mathematics.

So, bearing that in mind, what is the difference? Well, machine learning is plainly and simply a subset of artificial intelligence. Artificial intelligence comprises *many* different respects and fields, such as machine learning, natural language processing, pathfinding, and similar concepts. Anything that has to do with a computer being able to process and make decisions based on given data is, in a way, artificial intelligence.

Machine learning, on the other hand, refers specifically to a subset of techniques, algorithms, and theory that aims to supply the computer with the ability to *enhance* its ability to recognize things and make decisions. Machine learning thereby is the subset of artificial intelligence which is focused specifically on the *building* of computer intelligence. For example, artificial intelligence may have to do with the component wherein the computer can learn to parse languages and words and derive meaning from it by finding keywords. However, teaching a computer to *learn* what the different parts of speech are, or to recognize one language from another, is most definitely an application of machine learning specifically.

So, with all of that said, what then is the difference between machine learning and *deep learning*? Deep learning, too, has become somewhat of a computer buzzword much like both artificial intelligence and machine learning have. It's tossed around all the time, but in it being tossed around, very little meaning is maintained, and very little is explained.

Don't worry, as this book continues, we are going to be covering *some* basic deep learning concepts in the chapters having to do with neural networks. You will be learning about deep learning in this guidebook, though perhaps not as much as you would in a book specifically about deep learning.

But that reassurance does little to actually tell you what deep learning is and how it differs from machine learning. Deep learning is simply one application of machine learning itself. Deep learning specifically is the use of the concept known as neural networks, whereby computers emulate systems of neurons, similar to those found in the brain, to learn and work. Neural networks have been around since the early days of artificial intelligence, but they've only started to be particularly useful in recent years as computers have become more and more powerful and capable. Now, they have the processing power to render the extremely complex algorithms required of something like neural networks.

We'll talk more about what neural networks are when we get to their specific subchapter, but for right now, just understand the difference between machine learning and deep learning, deep learning simply being a subset of machine learning. Deep learning is just one form of the broad discipline of machine learning, just like machine learning is just one form of the broad discipline of artificial intelligence.

In this way, you can picture the three as forming somewhat of a hierarchy. Artificial intelligence is the broadest form, encompassing the most topics. Machine learning is just one form of artificial intelligence, and deep learning is just one form of machine learning. By extension, deep learning is just one form of artificial intelligence.

With that, we've covered much of the difference between the three. Hopefully, that helps you to have a firmer understanding of the three different disciplines and the differences between them. In the chapters to follow, we're going to be exploring machine learning and, in part, deep learning. Though deep learning isn't the entire point of this book, and as a result we aren't going to be digging super deeply into it, it is nonetheless an important part of machine learning and so we are going to spend a bit of time covering it - as well as *numerous* other topics along the way.

Reflection Questions

- What is the hierarchy of artificial intelligence?
- In what ways does deep learning differ from machine learning?
- In which contexts does machine learning shine? Where is it not so useful?

Chapter 3:
Machine Learning Workflows

"Some people call this artificial intelligence, but the reality is this technology will enhance us. So instead of artificial intelligence, I think we'll augment our intelligence." – ***Ginni Rometty***

If you want to start working with machine learning then it's best that you start to outline some machine learning workflows. These will define the manner and rate at which you're able to get work done in terms of machine learning.

So, what exactly is a machine learning workflow? A machine learning workflow can be defined as every element that plays into the actual development of technologies which use machine learning and the manner in which those technologies are implemented.

However, workflows in the contexts of technological workplaces tend to be divided into various steps. These steps allow teams and office environments to work together in order to make strong machine-learning based systems. These steps can take many different forms, but this chapter specifically is going to be focused mainly around the idea of working with the most common version: a five-step form of machine learning workflow.

The first step is the development of some kind of plan. This may seem like a no-brainer, but this is one of the most crucial parts of the whole process. Whether you're working with a team or on your own, this is an important part of the whole process of developing a machine learning solution. This is the point at which you pinpoint the problem in question and determine that there might be a particularly useful solution based in the disciplines of machine learning.

At this point in the process, you want to identify what your issue is, and then crystallize a method by which you can fix it with machine learning. This is the point at which you'll also develop your machine learning infrastructure.

What I mean by this is deerining what the programming needs and computing needs for your solution are. Some languages are better than others for certain purposes. For general data analysis the language R is very popular, and the language Python also has quite a bit of use. For things that are more performance-heavy or intensive, you may want to instead use C++. Every popular language at this point has a pretty large and worthwhile machine learning API or library that you can likely make use of. Some are better for various purposes than others.

At this point you also want to look into other people who have tackled similar problems and try to follow a similar path to what they did, or at least review their personal methodology and structure and see how you can adjust it to fit your own program and technology.

Afterward, what you're going to want to do is solidify your measure of *success*. What can be seen as good enough and having "completed" the project? Is it being able to implement something that can predict with a certain level of accuracy? Is it something that is able to review prior data and make reasonable assumptions based off that data with a high degree of accuracy? Is it some certain return on performance, e.g. accurate predictions with a minimal system impact? These are things you need to determine at this point.

Additionally, you may wish to do a study on the relevant information and try to look ahead for any potential risk that is inherent in the project. Be properly prepared and ahead of the curve for these.

Eventually, you're going to find yourself at step 2; step 2 is the step where you look into how feasible the project as a whole is and examine whether or not you can mitigate risk. This is the chance to see if a project is *worth it* before you actually start pouring your resources into it.

At this point, you're firstly going to be examining any data that you have to work with and then examining whether the data is good or not. You're also going to be trying to determine how suitable the data that you have is for various machine learning algorithms and try to determine if it's actually fit for what you're wanting to do.

You want to outline the general run of your program's architecture, and try to figure out various different approaches that you can use in order to solve the problem. This is the point at which you're also going to want to build a few basic different machine learning models and try to work with data in a basic way before specifically trying to tweak the system. All that you're trying to do is determine whether or not the models are adequate for everything that you're trying to do. You aren't trying to specifically hone or make them work perfectly for your data or purposes.

Eventually, you make your way to step 3. At step 3, you're trying to fully train whatever your algorithm and model is to fit your data. This process is based around training your model and fine-tuning it. You're wanting, by the end of step 3, to have all of your machine learning logic finalized, all of your equations and algorithms fine-tuned, and you're essentially wanting to have some sort of usable software that you can treat as the basis of the rest of your process. Step 3 doesn't require a whole lot of explanation because this step is basically just making use of other things that we've described in this book.

After step 3, you land on step 4. During step 4, you take your model online and deploy it to all necessary users. At this point, you keep a close eye on your program and watch how predict patterns grow and progress. This part of the equation involves keeping a careful and watchful eye over everything and being sure it all plays out like you're wanting it to.

After all of that, you're at step 5. Step 5 is simply letting your model live and then making any adjustments as necessary and trying to keep it all on track. You maintain your model, try to figure out the root of any problems that *do* happen, keep track on their statistics and any relevant user-based information, and maybe retrain your model if it ever comes to be necessary.

This is the basis for all major machine learning workflows. While there are some that are a bit more in-depth than this one, they all will follow this general schema in trying to make them work and trying to put out a usable and finite product. This is the basis of everything else you do. Understand and treat it as such.

Reflection Questions

- What is the basis of step 3? Can you rephrase it in one sentence?
- What languages are better for what purposes in machine learning? Do additional research if necessary; this answer is foundational to a lot of other things that you'll do.
- What stage is dedicated to figuring out whether or not your model is viable?

Chapter 4: About Computer Learning (Supervised, Unsupervised, Reinforcement)

"Artificial intelligence would be the ultimate version of Google. The ultimate search engine that would understand everything on the web. It would understand exactly what you wanted, and it would give you the right thing. We're nowhere near doing that now. However, we can get incrementally closer to that, and that is basically what we work on." — ***Larry Page***

Having discussed how to build up and then implement your machine learning workflow, we're now going to spend some time talking about the concepts which are actually *behind* machine learning. In this chapter, we're going to be covering how computer learning works as well as what the *three major types of computer learning* are.

So, let's start by taking a second to think about what machine learning really is. How do computers learn? Machine learning can be separated into numerous different categories, which essentially define the ways in which machine learning can be understood and applied in different contexts. There are five categories, and these categories define how different sorts of problems can be solved using machine learning.

The first category of use is ***classification***. Classification refers to using machine learning to classify things based on certain *categoristics* and using what the machine learns in the process of said categorization to categorize future things in a similarly intuitive manner. Machine learning through classification is therefore about teaching the computer how to categorize things through recognizing certain qualities and then placing it, based on those qualities, into a category or classification that has already been defined. More advanced classification systems can also create their own subclassifications or new classifications altogether.

The second category is ***regression***. Regression in machine learning is about analyzing data points algorithmically and then using your analysis as a starting point by which you can make numerical predictions. Numerical predictions essentially will allow you to use the data already presented to create a new number based on those previous events.

The third category of use is ***similarity*** or ***anomaly***. The use of this category in machine learning refers to the ability to either detect similarities or anomalies, which I suppose is somewhat self-explanatory. The concept of similarity refers to either identifying or classifying the concept and then using that to retrieve things which are similar in nature. This can be done with or without classification, but identification is an important part of the process, one way or another. The concept of anomaly refers to looking at standard procedures and then looking for *deviations* from those procedures. In essence, it's the opposite of similarity. Instead of looking for things which *are* similar, it seeks out things which are *not* similar and are therefore anomalous. A good example would be cheat detection systems in games which seek out bizarre behavior on the user's end, and then use those to infer that the user is cheating.

The fourth category is ***ranking***. Ranking involves using machine learning to reflexively order and predict what is the most relevant in correlation to a given user input. Ranking, therefore, is essentially for taking something and then using that as a starting point. All relevant data will be reflected for retrieval, and after being selected for this retrieval, they will be categorized based on what is most relevant to the user. The one (or ones) that the user select(s) will then be used to improve the algorithm based on the content and data of their selections in correlation with the given input query.

The fifth and final category is a ***sequential prediction***. The idea of sequential prediction is essentially looking at trends within a current series and then attempting to guess what the next thing should be. Again, the system will do so in a standard and algorithmic manner and will generally be modulated and further trained in response to the user's response, if such a thing is allotted for.

These are the primary use categories for machine learning and are, thereby, descriptions of the problems for which machine learning presents itself as the most adequate solution. These use categories may sound like they overlap quite a bit; that's pretty much because they *do*. For example, the data and process which presents itself as a solution to one problem will often work similarly for yet another problem. Moreover, they will sometimes feed off each other. For example, the numerical predictions which are returned through regression may actually provide a useful foundation for ranking data.

The goal of looking at these five methodologies for machine learning is simply to provide a sound foundation of theory to help you with approaching machine learning problems in your own way. Remember, these can be mixed and matched as you need, and you'll discover in your workflow that there are many cases where you're going to need to do just that. But by classifying these and breaking them into separate categories, it becomes easier to analyze them of their own merit and then work with them accordingly. It will greatly aid you in the pursuit of finding something.

But, beyond those methodologies, there are three different key forms of machine learning. This chapter from here on out is going to be about learning what these are, understanding how they work, and understanding how they apply to the key tenets of machine learning.

We've already learned that machine learning is essentially a manner by which a computer can learn patterns and make algorithmic determinations to chart future courses for its activity, or otherwise make predictions. We've also learned that to do this, computers need data. The more data computers have for working with, the more accurate predictions they can make regarding future information.

It's through these information flows that computers can analyze given data and come to conclusions. Imagine a piece of software which can determine whether there is a face in a picture. This is a marvel of modern technology, and we tend to undervalue how complex of an operation this can actually be. What's happening under the surface is the computer has enough data to work with, so there's an extremely advanced set of algorithms running. These algorithms look at a picture and compare to all the data sets that the computer has ever had and determines if the properties of a given image match the properties of images which have faces in them by comparing features of the image. For instance, where lines are drawn, where the colors are parallel with those that are the color of skin, where the shapes of eyes are congruent with those pictures of eyes that the computers have worked with before, and so forth. Using all this data and comparing the current image, the software can profile where the face may be if there is one. With more information, even more, attributes can be determined. For example, software could be written that would be able to detect the color of somebody's eyes.

All these incredible assumptions and conclusions are possible because the computer has a massive reserve of data and can work with and make determinations from. The process of letting the computer work with information, make automatic determinations and "learn" about the implications of certain attributes of data, in correlation to other data points, is what we ultimately know as *machine learning*. This is, therefore, the best definition that we've been able to develop throughout this whole book. For obvious reasons, this field has a huge amount of relevance in respect to things like data analysis, prediction, classification, and all the other problems we've talked about at being able to solve.

For a computer, learning is the creation of an algorithm and comparative method using existing data. There are three different primary ways in which this type of learning can take place. These are *supervised learning*, *unsupervised learning*, and *reinforcement learning*. The next few chapters of this book are going to focus on these and their respective implications and implementations in-depth.

Let's start by looking at supervised learning. What exactly is supervised learning? Supervised learning is essentially when you feed input to the program that you've developed with some sort of target data. The goal of this particular program is to find some sort of correlation between the input data and the target which you provide.

Supervised learning, therefore, is when you have some sort of data, and you're also providing the target. The program may simply attempt to form a bridge between the provided data and the provided target. This code then, algorithmically, attempts to find some sort of commonality between all the input data and their connections to the provided targets, such that the program can algorithmically use these associations and functions to determine from future input data what the targets may be. In this way, you can use given data to build some sort of machine learning system that can make future predictions.

Unsupervised learning, on the other hand, *doesn't* have a target provided. Unsupervised machine learning consists solely of input data. Therefore, there is no set of targets for x to correspond to necessarily. As opposed to supervised learning where somebody is telling the program, hands-on, what data should correlate to what, unsupervised lacks this *supervisor*. The algorithms that you develop for the program are completely and totally responsible for deducing what the nuances of the given sets of data are, without necessarily needing human interaction.

In terms of unsupervised learning against supervised learning, the nuances and differences can be rather clear. The primary difference is that supervised learning requires there be a human at the helm, telling the program what answers are correct, and which targets correspond to which data. It is through this correction that supervised machine learning can actually self-correct its algorithms and analysis procedures, and therefore, become better at predicting changes in data.

The last major form of machine learning is *reinforcement learning*. Reinforcement learning is based on a machine or program learning how things work through the process of trial and error, and then reviewing outcomes and using that to internalize certain processes. For example, if a machine were given two options, option A and option B, and option A was found to have a negative consequence, the machine would learn that it should take the path involving option B instead. This is a vast simplification, but the implications of this highly advanced artificial intelligence methodology are many.

By explicating and forming a basis for understanding these different methods of machine learning, we can start to understand the mechanism behind *all* forms of machine learning: data and reactions to data. However, the key difference between how humans learn and how machines learn is that humans are able to respond and react to data intuitively. We have built-in standards for responding to different events. Computers have to be taught the meaning of certain events; they don't have an inherent understanding of events or positive or negative necessarily. They have to instead be told what different markers mean and how they should interpret them.

This is why machine learning is so complicated, so in demand, so critical, and ultimately, so important. A person who truly understands machine learning understands, in some capacity or another, not just machine learning but also how the brain itself *works* and could offer insights into human understanding. Their understanding of data science, too, offers an incredible opportunity for prediction and more accurate interpretations of numerical insights that humans could easily miss.

The thing about computers is that they are perfect insofar as we make them perfect. They will always keep data we give to them, and they will always recall that data. Computers cannot, by definition, forget data; it is permanent, as long as it isn't corrupted. As a result, computers are actually far better at learning than we are, in a sense. This also comes with drawbacks, however; the utter complexity of a worthy computer-based learning system scales exponentially with the complexity of its goals. Therefore, while something that can simply analyze the stock market and make predictions based on former data about where a given stock may be headed next, is simple in a relative sense. Something that is capable of parsing more and more variables and situations becomes increasingly difficult as the programmer has to account for more deviance, more situational complexity, more algorithmic complexity, and so forth.

I guess what I'm saying here is that machine learning is incredibly important, and what's more important to understand than anything else is that the sky is the limit. We are only limited by the ability of our computer systems and our own personal ability to program different things into a computer. You've taken an excellent first step toward a very lucrative and rewarding hobby or career by picking up this book. The next few chapters are going to be based around really digging into these different forms of learning that we've covered within this chapter, and analyzing them in an algorithmic sense, as well as learning the different parts of their application and trying to figure out what makes them tick. By the end of the next few chapters, you're going to have a firm understanding of the three main different forms of machine learning and feel adequately ready to actually start studying the applications of machine learning and how it works.

Reflection Questions

- Why is machine learning necessary?
- Why has machine learning gotten more efficient and effective?
- In what ways do machines differ from human brains?

Chapter 5:
Supervised Learning

"Nobody phrases it this way, but I think that artificial intelligence is almost a humanities discipline. It's really an attempt to understand human intelligence and human cognition." – ***Sebastian Thrun***

In the former chapter, we spent quite a while going over the differences between the three main forms of learning in machine learning. This chapter is going to be spent going over the specific methodology of *supervised learning* and how it can be applied. In the process, we're going to be assessing numerous different methods and algorithms to build a firmer understanding of machine learning in general and especially supervised learning.

So, first off, let's review our definition of *supervised learning*. We learned in the previous chapter that supervised learning deals with having both a set of data that is provided, as well as a set of targets which this data correlates to. The intent of the supervised learning process is to build a function by which the input data x may be correlated with relative accuracy to the target data y.

This could perhaps be best described in terms of the following relationship:

$Y = f(X) + E$

Where ***Y*** is the end result of the function or the prediction and ***X*** is the input of the function and the data. ***f(X)*** refers to the function which actually takes *X* into account and morphs it in some way to predict *Y*. The key of supervised machine learning is that *Y* and *X* are both given; the point, then, is for the computer to figure out a means in which it may connect *X* and *Y* through the function *f(X)* and the degree of error ***E***.

Supervised machine learning operates largely off the use of labeling in data, which is assigning and classifying data based on your *Y* to give a means by which *X* may be expected and paradigmatically interpreted. This is run through an algorithm specifically tailored toward machine learning.

There are two primary focuses of supervised learning which we've discussed before but will be diving into in a little bit more depth now. These are *regression* and *classification*. As a reminder, regression serves as a means by which one may predict numeric values for data; classification is analyzing a data set and then being able to determine its *Y* value, then classifying it into groups based off its *Y* label.

This is, of course, easier said than done (and it's not quite easily said, which is saying something in and of itself!), but there is a relatively simple way of looking at it. You can look at supervised machine learning as having two major components: first, there is the *training* component, then there is the *testing* component.

The training component is centered around the program learning the prediction function *f(X)* given a set of data. This data must have both the *Y* and the *X* value. The testing component, on the other hand, involves yet another set of data where the program is not fed a specific *Y* value or label. The testing component is intended to predict a *Y* value using the modeled *f(X)* algorithm from the training component.

Over the rest of the chapter, we're going to be breaking down the different methods of supervised learning and how they apply overall to the field of machine learning, as well as how you can use these models to achieve the goals of regression and classification.

Parametric/Non-Parametric Algorithms

The most basic form of supervised learning, and the easiest to explain is the development of mathematical algorithms to do different things. These are based largely around mathematics and will adjust in correlation to the data which you present the algorithms with.

These algorithms are both parametric and *non*-parametric. The difference in these is that parametric functions follow a very strict and obvious pattern; parametric functions work by assuming regularity within the data. That is, parametric functions assume that there is a functional numeric relationship between the *X* values and the *Y* values and, moreover, that this numeric relationship can be deduced mathematically.

Non-parametric algorithms, on the other hand, focus on finding connections between *X* and *Y* values in a *non-functional* way; they assume no statistical *and* functional numeric connection between given values, and instead, are focused solely on finding a statistical connection between them that is *not* able to be deduced into a function.

The difference between the two is that non-parametric functions have a broader set of applications. They don't have to work with data that is necessarily based on a given function, and as a result, can fit into more tight spaces and have a far more flexible model than parametric functions do. However, at the same time, the fact that parametric algorithms follow a numeric standard and assume normality and regularity within the numbers can be quite a good thing when this is actually *true* because it means that predictions can be reduced numerically and, therefore, are quite likely to be accurate. On the other hand, since non-parametric functions aren't working within a given standard numerical function *f(x)* to get *Y*, they're more so based around finding connections between an unknown *X* and any surrounding *X* values to determine what the *Y* might be.

This section is going to be looking at a couple of different models for these kinds of algorithms. First, we're going to be looking at logistic and linear regression, which are two extremely important forms of *parametric algorithms*. Then we're going to be looking at *k-nearest neighbor* and *decision tree* algorithms which will give you a solid foundation of understanding in terms of *non-parametric* algorithms.

Linear Regression

The first algorithm that we're going to look at is *linear regression.* Linear regression is simple in concept, and it's a bit of a no-brainer. However, the actual application in computer science and artificial intelligence can be tricky, so we're going to look at it from that perspective and break it down a bit.

All parametric methods assume that there are set parameters within a mathematical function by which a correlation may be drawn between input data and output data. Let's call our input and output data in *algorithmic explanations* as *i* and *o,* respectively. From here, when we refer to *X* and *Y*, we are referring to those as data points on a 2D plane.

Linear regression assumes that there is a linear relationship between the input *i*, and the output *o*. Therefore, linear regression assumes that for any unknown *o*, we can reasonably predict *o* as a function of *i*, in congruence with the way that all currently known data works in terms of *i* and *o*. Linear regression works by creating what is commonly known as a *line of best fit* amongst input samples, and then from this, assuming that future predictions will roughly follow the line.

So, what we're assuming the data would be is:

$o = y\text{-}intercept + slope(i) + e$

In this model, since this is an expansion of our previous algorithm:

$o = f(i) + e$

We can presume that we're trying to find two parameters for this function: the *Y-intercept* and the *slope of the function* which best correlates to *i*, to produce output *o*.

We can run our data and our equation through a learning algorithm to try to come up with some sort of line of best fit. Once the line of best fit has been discovered, we need to come up with a function that will tell us how to measure how accurate our program is. Then, we need to find what we can do to make it even more accurate than it already is.

With a line of best fit, we can look at the prediction at each point by our learning algorithm, then look at the difference between that and the actual point. Then, you square this difference. Do this for all the different data points and then sum them up, then divide by two times the number of data points, like so:

sum of $(o*x + i) - y)^2 / 2n$

From here, you can minimize your results using standard calculus to find the best parameters for your algorithm $o = f(i) + e$.

However, sometimes you can't just minimize if the function above is sufficiently complex. In these cases, you're going to want to use what is best known as *gradient descent*. You do this by simplifying your function, so it's only in terms of $f(o, i) = c$, where c is the *cost* of the function, or how incorrect the prediction is. You can find the derivative of this parameter in both directions. Find the direction in which the total loss goes *down* from some example parameters, and then keep going in that direction until you actually find where the loss is the least that it could possibly be. Once you do that, you're all good to go, and you'll have minimized the function.

Minimizing is the most important part of parametric functions because your parametric functions are all about their *parameters*. If you manage to find the best parameters for the function, then you'll have found the best possible predictive function for your given data.

This isn't always the case, though.

Parametric Problems

Sometimes, in the pursuit of writing a really great solution, you'll have some problems actually constructing good and worthwhile paradigms for prediction. There can be several reasons for this, and it's important that we start to go over them now, that way you have some idea of how to deal with them when the time does eventually come.

So, think about it for a second - when you're modeling a predictive function, what are you really trying to do? What is your end goal? Well, your end goal is that whenever you parse some new data with that function, you are able to reliably estimate what the value might be based on your previous data. So, what would be an example of something that could get in the way of this? It would be something that actually *reduces* the ability of your predictive model to accurately represent the data in question and make solid predictions that are realistic and congruent with the data that you've already given.

There is such a thing as *bias-variance tradeoff*. Bias refers to the ability of a model to represent the data in question with a model. An extremely high bias means that the model doesn't fit the data well. Variance, on the other hand, refers to how well a model responds to the fluctuation of deviation within your model. A model that has high variance fits the given data well.

Within these exist two separate phenomena that can both affect your graph: *overfitting* and *underfitting*.

Overfitting refers to your graph having too low a bias and too high a variance. The bias component means that the model explains the given data extremely effectively - it fits the data to a tee. Variance means much the same - the model represents the data well, and there is a lot rate of error between the predictions that the model makes, and the actual data points.

The goal is to have both your bias and your variance be low. In this case, your model would not only approximate the existing data well but also serve as a good predictor for future data. When data is overfitted, the model is *too* "good" at fitting the existing data. This might make it difficult for future trends to be predicted, because the model which connects all of your points may not reflect the *actual* pattern that is happening. Even though it is correct at every predictive point compared to the actual data, it doesn't actually make good predictions in the future because the model is too complex for some meaningful parametric data to be extrapolated from it for future reference.

Underfitting, on the other hand, refers to your graph having *too high* a bias and too *low* a variance. In this case, the model isn't complicated enough. The bias fact means that the margin of error is too high, and the fact that the variance is too low means that the model doesn't change enough to accommodate all of the data pieces. It fails to accurately capture the structure of the data points.

These are the two biggest problems in the design of models that you need to be aware of because they can drastically throw off your predictions. Being aware of what they are, how they work, and why they happen is the best way to be prepared against them when the time comes.

Logistic Regression

Logistic regression is the other main form of parametric modeling that we're going to cover. It works pretty similarly to linear regression, but it applies what's called the *sigmoid function*, which in turn ensures that the function will output a number between 0 and 1.

The logistic regression algorithm can be used for both the classification of items. It allows you to determine whether something belongs to some other thing given the existence (or non-existence) of certain properties.

Recall the formula for our linear regression algorithm. Logistic regression essentially aims to take that linear regression algorithm and make it work within the context of a value from 0 to 1 based around probability, where a number closer to 1 indicates that an event will happen and a number closer to 0 indicates that an event is *less* likely to happen.

I'm going to spare you the math component of this since libraries by and large already allot for logistic regression. The initiated would be advised to look into sigmoid functions and understand how they work. Logistic regression is just a linear regression equation applied within the context of a sigmoid function.

Non-Parametric Algorithms - K-Nearest Neighbors

We've already discussed briefly what a non-parametric algorithm is. It's what you can use to build more complex and dynamic algorithms for use with data that expand a bit beyond the normal algorithmic complexity of standard mathematical models. If your data doesn't seem to have clear, correlative connections, this might be the thing that you want to use.

The principle remains the same between parametric and non-parametric algorithms, sensing patterns in data to predict what another element of that data may actually be. Adjusting in accordance with this is the name of the game with non-parametric algorithms because they don't have explicitly programmed mathematical data models to work with. Rather, they work with the properties of the data around a given thing.

Perhaps the best example of this is the *k-nearest neighbor's* algorithm, often shortened to *k-NN*. What k-nearest neighbors do is it looks at the data points closest to the point that you're trying to predict, and then uses that data to assume what the thing is. The assumption is that whenever you have one piece of data near in location to other pieces of data, there's a pretty good chance that whatever that piece of data is, it is related to, or identical in classification to the other pieces of data.

Imagine a graph with clusters of dogs, cats, and horses. If these were interspersed throughout the graph with only slight noise and variance, such that clusters were, for the most part, reminiscent of their primary class (e.g., a cluster of dogs would have mostly dogs; a cluster of cats would have mostly cats) and that things of a certain class, despite some intermingling due to the graphical noise, would tend to mingle together. You would assume that an unknown animal that was surrounded by three dogs and one cat was most likely a dog, correct?

This is the logic of k-nearest neighbors. It assumes that the classification of an object within a data set will be the same as those pieces of data near it, or that those pieces of data could be used to extrapolate/predict things about the piece of data in general. (For example, in pursuit of a prediction of a mystery number surrounded by three “high” numbers and one “low number”, it may be assumed that the mystery number is a high number, and then it may be assumed that the value of that mystery number is an average of the other three *high* numbers. This would give a reasonable prediction.)

You set *k* as the means of defining the *scope* of the algorithm in question. For example, if you were to set the scope at 5, then the algorithm would seek the five nearest neighbors to your data point and then compare them to achieve the probable classification or value of the target data point.

This raises the question - how does one define how near something is to something else? There are a few different methods by which you can do this. The two that we're going to focus on here are Euclidean and Manhattan distances. These are two parallel and different forms of distance that can give you different ideas of how far things are from one another.

Euclidean distances can be thought of as the distance from one thing to another in terms of a straight line. It draws from the definition of the hypotenuse of a triangle and seeks to find the distance between two things in Euclidean space. It's expandable to any dimension, though.

Recall, for a moment, the Pythagorean theorem:

$a^2 + b^2 = c^2$

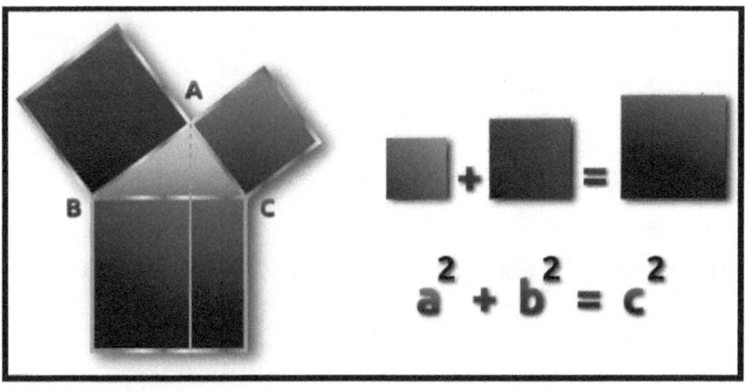

Through algebra, we can deduce that the length of our hypotenuse, with the *x* and *y* distance between the two points treated as the sides of the right triangle, would be like so:

$c = \text{sqrt}(a^2 + b^2)$

To find the differences between these locations, we must subtract them from one another:

$c = \text{sqrt}((x_2 - x_1)^2 + (y_2 - y_1)^2)$

Were there an additional dimension, we could actually extend this to whatever dimension it was. For example, if we were dealing with data that held three different dimensions, we could calculate the distance of one data point from another like so:

$c = \text{sqrt}((x_2 - x_1)^2 + (y_2 - y_1)^2 + (z_2 - z_1)^2)$

In essence, you can understand it as the sum of some number *x* to the *nth* dimension:

$c = \text{sqrt}(\text{sum}((x(n)_2 - x(n)_1)^2))$

This yields an incredibly useful distance between any two given points that you can use to find the nearest data points to your given target data, and then come up with some sort of useful conclusion.

The other kind of distance is *Manhattan* distance. This is simply the sum of the difference between the coordinates:

$$c = (x_2 - x_1) + (y_2 - y_1)$$

Expanded to however many dimensions you find yourself needing, of course.

You can test multiple different values of *k* and then compare them against one another using your test data. In doing this, you can compare the prediction to the level of error. You can then know what value of *k* to use by picking the one which has the lowest rate of error.

There are some natural problems to this at extremely high scales; extremely high numbers of *k* can yield extremely useless data because it's working with too much data to have an adequately small sample size. However, this methodology has quite a bit of usage in real-world applications.

For example, because of how flexible it is, in situations where data is constantly entered, and the prediction model depends solely upon the existing data pool, this method excels. It can make predictions based off the already existing data and update pretty much automatically with new information since all you're doing is feeding the system more data anyway.

Additionally, there are some real-life situations where, knowing what the nearest thing to something else are, will *realistically* give you a very solid prediction. For example, gas prices; the gas prices of one gas station is likely to be similar to those of any gas stations within a three-mile radius. By taking this estimate, you can have a reasonable prediction of the cost of gas of both a given area as well as the predictive price of gas at a given station.

Decision Trees

The other major non-parametric algorithm that you should know is the use of *decision trees*. Decision trees are used to make solid estimations about future data in a given situation based on a sequence of different decisions.

Decision trees are essentially about understanding linear paths to come to conclusions based on the typical method of those linear paths. Decision trees, therefore, are good at making predictions regarding population-based data. One could look at a survey of the population in terms of their socioeconomic data. For instance, one could use this to make determinations on whether they are college-educated and whether they *completed* that college education. This would allow us to model and predict whether someone, based on their socioeconomic status, is likely to attend a university and finish out at their university.

The goal is to ask questions about each data point and then separate them in ways that can maximize the amount of information that you're getting from every question or split in the tree. For example, in terms of college education, socioeconomic status is a good place to start because people of a higher socioeconomic status tend to be more likely to have attended and completed college. The fact is that the more specialized jobs tend to draw bigger incomes, and specialization implies education.

The goal is that, at every split in the tree, you're maximizing the amount of information that you're gaining through the split. Asking socioeconomic status means that we have much more pertinent information to work with, and that there is likely to be more consistency amongst our data pieces (e.g., people who don't attend college are more likely to be nearer and grouped with those who also didn't attend college, with fewer being grouped with those who *did*.)

You can build up a decision tree through a large set of data and decision splits, then train your algorithm with that. Moreover, you can train your algorithm with several different decision trees that you create using the same data. This sort of training and retraining will give your algorithm and software a huge amount of different individual pieces of data to work with, which can make a massive difference in how advanced and capable your algorithm is.

The use of many different decision trees will enable you to have a far more capable predictive algorithm. Ideally, in the creation of this sort of algorithm, your decision tree algorithms will also be pulling random samples from the data to better their trees and make them more separate, which reduces the chance of your predictive model having too high a variance and then overfitting to the data.

With that, we've covered the other major non-parametric method for supervised learning.

Support Vector Machines

Support vector machines work similarly to the other parametric algorithms and work to do the same thing that logistic regression does, and also does so with minimal impact on the system's running performance compared to logistic regression. In both cases, they are roughly the same as far as system impact and what they can *do*.

Support vectors are essentially about taking data points and finding a line that separates them as cleanly as possible. If a target data point falls on one side or another of this line based on the currently given algorithms, there is a good chance that it would be classified as that, so we give it the classification of the side which it falls on.

If you imagine two clusters of data on a graph that are separated by a line, it's not too hard to imagine the different ways in which that line could actually *exist*. However, there is only one optimal way to draw this line, so that the space between the line and the clusters of data is maximized. The more space on either side of the line means the less chance that something could mistakenly fall on the wrong side. This distance between the dividing line and the data points is referred to as the *margin*, and you're trying to make this margin as large as possible.

To find the best line, you're going to need to maximize your margins. You can usually perform your optimization algorithm with the data points on either side of your drawn line that are closest to it. (Or your plane if working in three dimensions.) These are called your *support* vectors, which is where the name of the method comes from.

This should give you the optimal line and the greatest margin for your data. Now, let's assume that for some reason your data isn't able to be separated very easily; what can you do?

There are two things that you can do here. First, you can open up your definition of separation so that more misclassifications are allowed on either side of the line. This makes it easier overall to work with the data in question, and it will allow you to separate it with more ease now that more margin for error is allowed with your learning algorithm.

The other thing that you can do is add a third dimension which will allow you to separate the data. This third dimension could be another data category, or it could be a manipulation of the first two data categories that produce a third data category. Regardless, the important thing is that you can create a new model which clearly delineates between your two classes if you decide that you need to separate your data through yet another dimension.

With that, we've covered support vector machines, which are the last major form of parametric or non-parametric machine learning.

Kernels

The kernel is a concept which commonly accompanies machine learning, especially support vector machines. Typically, kernels refer to *radial basis function kernels*. Kernels offer a manner by which you can measure the similarity between two different data points. The radial basis function kernel specifically allows you to measure the similarity between two things as a measure of how far from one another they are. This returned number is between one and zero, with one being the max and zero being the minimum.

Zero indicates that the two are not similar at all, while one indicates that they are. One parameter, or gamma, allows you to define the distance at which one point is considered *too far* from another to be similar to it through the lens of the RBF kernel.

Reflection Questions

- How do kernels and support vector machines work together?
- What are the perks of linear regression vs. logistic regression and vice versa?
- What is the best way to build a decision tree model, provided you have the processing power?

Chapter 6: Unsupervised Learning

"Artificial intelligence is growing up fast, as are robots whose facial expressions can elicit empathy and make your mirror neurons quiver." — ***Diane Ackerman***

The goal of unsupervised learning runs parallel to that of supervised learning. Supervised learning is largely about programming something so that it will be able to take given labels and then make predictions about given data sets based on those labels as they apply to an *X* data set. Unsupervised learning is based around having a bunch of data that *hasn't* been classified, labeled, or otherwise given some sort of properties which describe and befit the data in question.

This is *not* easy. Essentially, you're trying to find structure in data without a predefined structure.

This can be difficult to do. There are two main methods by which one can practice *unsupervised learning* - clustering, and dimensionality reduction. Both of these are useful in their own ways and have many applications.

Clustering is, more or less, the idea of grouping data points together based off attributes which are similar. The algorithmic method for doing so can be fairly complex or fairly simple depending on the data and the intensity of the clustering.

Dimensionality reduction, on the other hand, is about *reducing* the traits and manners by which the data may be seen, while keeping some sort of structure to the data and allowing the data to continue to be valuable.

Unsupervised learning is potentially the more useful in terms of future applications as opposed to supervised learning, because of the much larger subset of applications that exist for it. It can apply to so many situations and, as computers get stronger and the algorithms get better, the various uses of unsupervised learning are only going to multiply.

For now, let's take a look at the two data manipulation techniques that actually define unsupervised learning.

Clustering

Clustering is simple in concept but can be carried out in many different ways. The goal of this section is to break down some of the different ways and build a greater appreciation for the ideas behind clustering in the first place. So, what is clustering?

Clustering stays true to its name; it's the grouping of data which is based on attributes that are deemed to be similar and are cut off by clear delineations. The logic is this: if you have six things, all of which have the same property specifications, and four of these things have some of those properties in common or are extremely similar in their expression of those specifications, while the other two are extremely similar in their own right, you probably have two distinct groups and subclassifications of the data just based on the information and properties provided.

These properties, for the record, are referred to as *dimensions*. Every piece of data has at least one dimension, and to be expressed graphically, must have at *least* two dimensions with more possible. We'll talk more about dimensions specifically in just a moment.

Clustering is based around analyzing these dimensions and then finding similarities between groups of data based on certain dimensions, then breaking those pieces of data off into their individual distinct groups.

The most popular form of clustering is *k-means clustering*. In *k-means clustering*, you're trying to break your data into a certain *k* number of groups. If you set *k* to be bigger, then there will be more groups that things are broken down into; a smaller *k* implies that there will be less groups.

The end goal of k-means clustering is the development of a bunch of different labels that point each target toward one of the groups that were created. These are what are fed back to you on your end, most of the time. These groups are based around pieces of data called *centroid. Centroids* are pieces of data which are designated as centroids through certain properties. These can be set up at random, or you can train an algorithm which will best separate the data at the cost of performance and time. Anyhow, from here, the rest of the data will gather toward the centroids that they are most similar to.

By the end of the k-means clustering algorithm, you'll have actually developed a clean delineation within your data into however many different groups that you've assigned. This is the most common form of clustering that you'll come across.

Dimensionality Reduction

Dimensionality reduction is about trying to take your data set and make it progressively less complex while also making sure that you aren't stripping it of any potentially useful information. This can be harder said than done. We're going to look at one primary form of dimensionality reduction known as *principal component analysis* here.

Principal component analysis is essentially about understanding what the most pertinent data points and vectors within a space of certain dimensions are. Remember, it's really only feasible to visualize up to the third dimension, after which it becomes much more difficult.

In essence, principal component analysis is about looking for commonalities within the presented data and then reducing it by a dimension while maintaining the variance of the overall data. The most significant points are those which contain most of the variance. The remapping of the equation leads to data which is dimensionally smaller but maintains the same essential shape and structure as the previous data. In this sense, you have essentially compressed the data.

Neural Networks

It's that time - it's time that we talk about one of the hardest concepts to work with in all of machine learning. It is also one of the most popular concepts, and it has been something we've been toying with for a long time, and only recently had the computer to start working with more emphatically. This concept is, of course, neural networks.

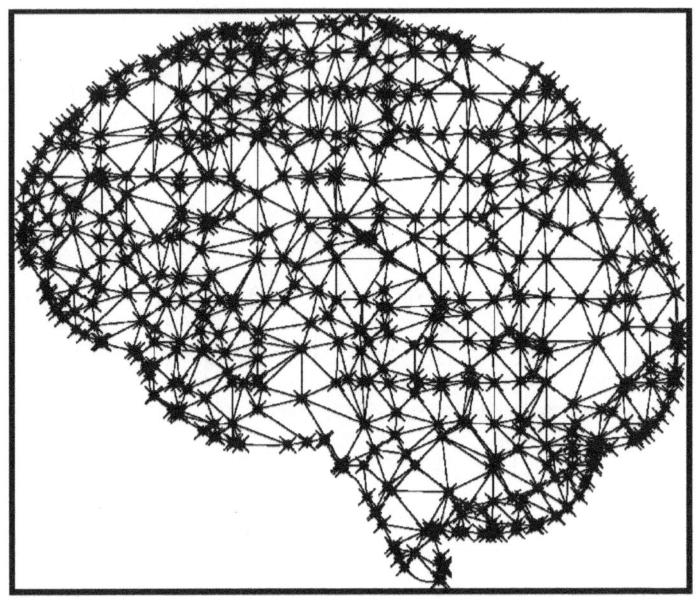

What are neural networks? Let's start with what a *neuron* is. A neuron, as you probably know, is the means by which the brain actually manages information (in short, anyway.) Powered by electrical charges, neurons are the small components of the brain that send signals to other parts of the brain. (Again, in short.)

The neural network is modeled off the biological networks that make up the brains of many different mammals. Neural networking is amazingly impressive and complex, and people who are adept with neural networking are highly in demand in the industry right now because of how powerful and complex it is.

The simplest truth is that absolutely gigantic 1,000-page textbooks are written about neural networks, and it would be impossible to truly cover all that there is to cover here. Instead, we're going to be covering a lot of the basics as well as how they correlate to deep learning and *why* they're so popular. From there, hopefully, you'll be able to extend and apply your knowledge in other ways.

So, let's start with our understanding of how neural networks work. Essentially, neural networks are a manner by which computers can use a ton of different pieces of information to make one finite decision. This decision-making process happens through a complex series of considerations regarding information called *layers*. Any deliberation that happens between the data being fed in and the prediction being fed out is known as a *hidden layer*.

Let's break this down so that it's a bit more abstract for a moment. How do neurons detect data? How does an actual brain recognize things within the world? Believe it or not, it's not through the holistic recognition of large pieces of information. For instance, when you see a car, you don't look at it as one whole piece and say *that is a car*. Maybe that's what you do internally, but in recognizing something, your brain is actually breaking down a bunch of small context clues that are all being picked up in different parts of your brain. These specific features are understood in terms of incredibly low-level features, which then build up to medium-sized features until finally working up to the highest level. So instead of seeing a car, you actually see other features - the shape and outline of its various features, which you then recognize as doors or side mirrors, which you then finally recognize as a car, which you then may finally recognize as a certain make or model of car. This process of recognition happens extremely quickly - almost instantaneously, in fact. And, in fact, if any of these things were to be found not to be the case that led up to you finally recognizing it as a car, you would not see it as a car. For example, if it didn't have wheels, but it had other features of a car, then you also noticed that it was sitting in the water, you would instead surmise that it was a boat.

The manner by which this immense net of recognition of small features building up into even bigger features, which then build up into even bigger features, is known as a *neural network.* Neural networks are incredibly good at what they do. In fact, neural networks are great because they can figure out literally *any function.*

Why is this useful? Because the real world involves a lot of change and a lot of variance. Things aren't always as simple as a linear equation, and other methods don't always account very well for breaks in this chain of linearity. Neural networks do, though. Neural networks do so very well, in fact, because they're able to adjust in accordance to various different phenomena and also take into account different variations in data.

This suits neural networking especially well to things which are fit for processing in a sophisticated manner. One example is image recognition. Image recognition is extremely hard to do reliably with a linear model.

Why is image recognition difficult to do with a linear model? Because things don't only have one orientation - they have *many* different orientations. They also have many different forms that they could take and can be any number of colors. For instance, a horse has a consistent set of features that distinguish it from a cat or a dog. However, the animals themselves may be any number of different breeds, colors, and so forth.

Now, with all of that said, why does this matter? Couldn't we theoretically just find an *average* example of an animal and then use this as a means to form a composite for what it *could* be? Can't that alone give us a predictive basis? Potentially, but only if we allowed for a unilateral method of image presentation. However, when you start to factor in additional orientations, it becomes messier to have a singular obvious output node that detects these features and then bases one conclusion or another off them.

Moreover, if you were to seek a way to actually stack these features on top of one another and test for them all at the same time - say, combining your different orientations of your "example" animal into one image - you end up with a very messy and hard to recognize depiction of an animal that doesn't do you any good as far as predictive analysis goes, in that real data is never going to actually match up to it.

So, we ultimately need something more comprehensive. We need something smarter. We don't just need pixel for pixel comparisons and probability matrices. What we need are neural networks.

Neural networks are basically a web of different detections and realizations about data. The essential way that they work is through the slow and steady activation of several different artificial neurons; the exact manner in which these artificial neurons activate will give an end prediction about what the object in question most likely is. A good and well-trained neural network will be able to make predictions with high levels of accuracy.

So, essentially, neural networks are about identifying small and concrete features in the data and then using those features to realize that there are more *abstract* ideas; the ideas get progressively more and more abstract until you have something at the end which is the abstract *idea* that you're predicting. The last layer in your neural network will be a set of all the different probabilities that the layer or layers prior had led up to.

Neural networks will gradually figure things out as you go, trying to increase the accuracy of the function as time goes on and automatically readjusting as it *learns*, which is, in a way, a form of unsupervised learning.

Hidden layers are the most crucial part of neural networks because they are where the magic happens. With even just one hidden layer, a neural network is already able to figure out what any mathematical function in data is. The more hidden layers you implement, the more abstract that features can get as you go, which will allow you to recognize (and, by extension, predict) more and more advanced sets of data as time goes on. Eventually, you can have a neural network that's such a tangled mess of different mathematics and code, that it's extremely difficult to interpret and you may not really know what's going on - this is known as *black-box,* and the state of trying to improve upon a black-box is known as *black-box optimization*. This is, ideally, something that you want to avoid at all costs because it massively removes you from the driver seat in terms of your neural network, and it makes it very difficult for you to properly internalize and understand what's going on within your data in the first place.

How good is neural networking? It's astoundingly good. With relatively small code bases, you can make very impressive things happen just by understanding the logic behind neural networks. Neural networks have seen expansion, too, with the advent of deep learning which has made neural networking incredibly popular.

Deep Learning

Deep learning is by and large the most common implementation of neural networks. It's the thing which has brought them all the spotlight lately, and the prime reason that people have started flocking to deep learning.

Deep learning allows a lot of really cool and specific implementations of neural networks such as image recognition or helping to translate text in a dynamic and more natural way than the former paradigm for translation. We'll be going into a huge number of other applications for machine learning in the chapter, specifically dedicated to the applications of machine learning, so don't worry about that. For now, we're just going to talk about deep learning, what it is, and *why* it's so useful.

Deep learning is essentially the process of using a very complex neural network to break things down into their components. These bigger concepts can be any number of things. For example, in the case of translation, it may be breaking down a sentence into smaller individual words and then building off *that* by looking at the other ways that people have used these words, or the correct ways they've translated in the past and so forth; all of which enable the computer to somewhat *learn* the structure of language and how language itself works. Instead of looking at words and sentences in a rigid way, the neural network will instead break constituent words and phrases down to their components and examine the sentence piece by piece.

Over time, the deep learning system will learn how to recognize different *parts* of speech, and then slowly adapt its paradigm so that it becomes *better* at doing so. Take the idiom "cut the cheese"; on its own, a translation system *without* deep learning that was trying to translate this phrase, might do so in a direct way because it wouldn't be able to recognize that this is a metaphorical part of speech. As a result, the phrase "cut the cheese" translated into French, for example, would be rendered *literally* as *couper le fromage*.

This, however, is not ideal for obvious reasons; language is an example of something that's always shifting around, and as a result, both language and translation make an excellent example of why and where deep learning shines. All languages have slightly different structures and features, and computers - unlike humans - lack the natural reasoning and linguistic capacities for determining what these languages are and breaking them apart. However, they can be trained to understand the basic *components* of language - noun phrases, verb phrases, adjectives, adverbs, idioms, subject phrases, object phrases, prepositions, and so forth - as well as understand *usage,* and how things fit together and are generally translated. They can then also keep a measure on how language *works in the living sense,* rather than just the literal sense. This is because it can keep tabs from *actual users* on how things translate from one language to another, backed up by external training data from people who know both their target language and origin language, perhaps even in a different context.

In some ways, deep learning and neural networks are innately connected. After all, deep learning implementations are generally just very large sets of neural networks. This also explains why deep learning has only recently come to the forefront: it's only within the last decade or so that computers have really started to have the processing power necessary to power multiple neural networks, and especially the processing power of the *average hobbyist or career programmer*. It doesn't matter that there are thousands of supercomputers; it is the billions of computers around the world that make an even *bigger* difference in terms of hobbyists and programmers being able to access them, tinker with neural networks and algorithms and constantly improve upon them. Processing power for the "average Joe" for much of recent history simply *didn't cut it*.

However, this isn't the case anymore. Computers nowadays are far more capable of handling the intense processing power required by things such as deep learning and heavily connected neural networks.

There's only so much that this book can teach you about neural networks within the scope that we've gotten to; the best way to learn about neural networks is really to start getting your hands dirty with them. There are a number of different tutorials online for different libraries, such as TensorFlow, that will allow you to get a feel for both neural networks and deep learning so that you can actually start applying those paradigms and making really cool, really smart software.

Reflection Questions

- What is the difference between neural networks and deep learning?
- What is the purpose of dimensionality reduction?
- How do you find the best *k* while clustering?

Chapter 7: Reinforcement Learning

"More data beats clever algorithms, but better data beats more data." — **Peter Norvig**

The models for machine learning that we've explored prior in the book have largely been focused on using pre-given data, sometimes even with labels, for prediction. Sometimes, however, this isn't the best route. Much like in real life, there are many times where the best route is actually based upon response to stimuli and through the process of cause and effect. The point of reinforcement learning is to cater to this specific process so that machines are able to learn in a fluid, dynamic manner rather than learning in a strictly data-based manner.

So, let's spend a little time talking about an example of reinforcement. Everybody knows the example of a kid not learning why they should never touch a hot stove until they, unfortunately, touch a hot stove. The kid then learns, "Oh, I really shouldn't touch a hot stove, I have very little to gain from that," and from there, they hopefully won't touch a hot stove ever again. This is the basis of reinforcement learning.

However, in actual applications, reinforcement learning is a little more complex than that. You can use reinforcement learning as a means to understand, for example, navigation toward a certain object. Let's say that you're a cat in a maze, and at the end of that maze, there's a big bowl of milk. Along the way, there are individual pieces of kibble, but along the way, you are trying to avoid stepping on mouse-traps. We could see this as tiered benefits, where the big bowl of milk is a big reward, the kibble is a small reward, and the mousetraps are a small penalty. You could also cluster the kibble in groups in some places while not in others.

After a little exploring, you would eventually find your way to a relatively small kibble cluster that you can eat. You could then keep coming back and eating kibble from this cluster, which gives you a relatively small reward each time. However, if you kept doing this, you'd never be aware that there were other kibble clusters that are potentially bigger within the maze. More than that, you may never decide to reach the end of the maze and get to your big bowl of milk.

So, in this case, what do you do? What you're working with, then, is what can be referred to as the trade-off between *exploration* and *exploitation*. Exploration is the state of actively seeking a greater reward even if it's not the best-known choice in any given position *p*, where you could already be exploiting a reward. For example, if you found a small kibble cluster and you started eating from it and exploiting it, it is from your position *logical* to keep exploiting that resource, because you have a guaranteed repeated small reward. However, this also requires acknowledging the fact that there may be a much better reward later on in the maze, were you to keep continuing on.

This is manifested through the *epsilon*. The *epsilon* is the probability that at any given moment, some agent will decide to act randomly instead of just acting in favor of reward based off what it has learned thus far. A higher epsilon indicates that more time will be spent exploring rather than focusing on what rewards are already known.

The movement of an agent being propelled by reinforcement learning can be standardized through the *Markov Decision Process*. A Markov Decision Process is basically a process where:

- any given location or position is considered a state,

- where each of these states has a different and finite array of actions it can undertake,
- connections between each of these states (usually rendered as movement but can, in the abstract, be anything that carries an agent from one state to another state),
- there are rewards for any given transition between states (even if this reward is zero, e.g., nothing happened in that transition),
- a coefficient between zero and one which allows someone to actually codify the perceived rewards of state transitions, whether those are immediate or whether they occur later, *and*
- a constantly updating algorithm which in one manner or another makes the overall history of the travels due to the fact that

all of the knowledge and the equations themselves are cumulative.

Reinforcement learning is rather simple at the conceptual level. However, the actual implementation of reinforcement learning through the Markov Decision Process can be quite difficult. The best way to get practice with this specific type of machine learning is to get your hands dirty with it. Reinforcement learning has its best applications in robotics and things which need to be able to learn dynamically. They don't have to literally be responding to their environment. Rather, they just need to have some sort of framework within, which they will either make mistakes or do the right thing and get rewarded. It is the notion of good and bad behaviors and correlated consequences which actually defines reinforcement learning, so any model which allots for these is an acceptable application.

Reflection Questions

- How should you define your epsilon throughout the program?
- How can you avoid your hypothetical cat taking from the same resource over and over?
- How can you implement positive and negative reinforcement?

Chapter 8: Best Practices in Machine Learning

"By far the greatest danger of Artificial Intelligence is that people conclude too early that they understand it." — ***Eliezer Yudkowsky***

In this chapter, we're going to lay out some of the best practices regarding machine learning. These are general skills that you can hone, to become much better at programming and specifically at programming machine learning applications. There is no one finite path to becoming an adept programmer, especially regarding machine learning; understand that before we continue with this chapter. However, there are a variety of things that you can do in a general sense that will improve your ability as a programmer in the *realm of machine learning,* and that will inspire people to work with you more often on more intensive projects.

Focus on One Discipline at a Time

Machine learning is comprised of numerous, different disciplines, as we've already discussed. Many people will particularly specialize, with time, in one particular discipline which happens to strike their fancy. For example, I particularly focus on the realm of natural language processing and the interactions between machines and human language, with an emphasis on both textual and audial recognition, as well as the structure and syntax of language.

Still, others will specifically focus on how they can improve neural networks algorithmically and extract the most information from this same structure, and enjoy the task of applying neural networks and deep learning to a variety of different situations to see if they can improve upon the methodology of application for deep learning.

More still are specifically into financial data analysis and the application of deep learning and machine learning to understand the world of finance and the patterns therein. These people tend to be more economically minded and will often go to work in the business industry.

Others yet are focused on the idea of self-driving cars and robotics and how these two categories can help improve the day-to-day life of humanity. They see artificial intelligence as an end goal and not necessarily as a thoroughfare and are therefore focused on the idea of growing artificial intelligence as a discipline. This would make computers smarter and more intuitive, and then develop those intuitions and rationalities into streamlined and efficient computer systems that have an impact on our everyday life.

There are so many different subsets and applications of machine learning, so many that your specific niche that you care about is going to have a lot of information and nuance to it. I would personally recommend that you try out several different projects from several different niches and see what kind of things you enjoy the most. For example, I personally don't enjoy working with data all *that* much, but the idea of helping computers to understand language and emotion is extremely interesting to me. There are also a number of people who are focused on the emulation of human neurological structures through computers, and many other disciplines still.

Note that when you specialize in artificial intelligence, you aren't just specializing in computers. This is the tricky part. No, the application of artificial intelligence and programming implies that you not only intimately understand the computer science aspect - what most makes computers tick, how to best manage memory - nor the statistical and mathematical aspect - finding algorithmic methodologies for functions f and then extrapolating them to entire data sets, finding the margins of a given line of regression, so on and so forth - but also the specific *space of application* for these. For example, what good is the idea of applying these structures to language if you don't understand linguistics? What good is it to extend our knowledge of machine learning to discover new drugs if you don't understand biochemistry? And so on. It's for this reason that, if you want to get extremely good with machine learning, you need to pick a subset, stick with it, learn it, and try to improve it. Jacks of all trades hardly make a real difference and are best relegated to patch-code and code maintenance - which is fine, if that's what you want to do.

Don't Reinvent the Wheel

You'll notice that through the course of this book, we've focused a lot on the raw *concepts* of algorithms and *a tiny bit* with the mathematical aspect, but we haven't rigorously focused on the applications of these algorithms within the context of code. That's because, for the most part, these algorithms have by and large been implemented.

It's a manner of rigor and self-reliance to develop your own machine learning libraries and machine learning algorithms, but it is for the most part unnecessary. There are a number of libraries out there such as TensorFlow, SciKit, and more that already have procedures established for working with datasets, performing common algorithmic operations, and then working with the data in question.

For a beginner machine learning book, it is simply *not necessary* to focus on the hard implementations of all of this logic. This is also because every library's interpretation of these ideas can be rather different. So, any code examples are:

1) Superfluous, or

2) Subject to change

Not to mention the variance between languages and libraries. (Code written in R will vary massively from code written in Python which therefore differs massively from code written in C++) Even drawing out solutions in pseudo code can be almost impossible for these types of problems without any sort of hard sample data.

The best thing to do is find a language and library that you like - I personally recommend something like Python due to the fact that there are a number of readily available machine learning libraries, and libraries for the display of this data like matplotlib - and then find a comprehensive tutorial for that library. And don't worry - with how popular machine learning is, there will be tutorials.

Earlier on in the book, I said that the best way to learn neural networks was by being hands-on, and that too much time on the specifics would be a pretty big waste of time. This holds true. The best thing to do is to get out there and get your hands dirty.

Work with Other Projects

There are a lot of people out there working with machine learning structures. A *whole lot.* One of the best things that you can do for yourself as a programmer is to get out there and start working with some of the code that these other people have written, and tinker with it yourself.

There are two reasons to do this. The first is that there is always a better programmer than you.

You can learn from other people's code every time you open it up and read it. This is how you're going to be able to gain a lot of skill. You'll also learn the APIs by seeing how other people work with them.

However, the other is that this is simply the best way to gain experience. Let's be honest, you're working in an extremely unfamiliar territory, and the documentation for any given library isn't always going to give you *all* the information that you need. In these cases, seeing other people use the code and implement things in ways other than the ways you may have thought of, can be of great help.

Those are the three best things you can do if you want to become a good machine learning programmer. By picking up these three best practices, you will be on the path to excellence. In the following chapter, we're going to look at applications of the things that we've covered so far in this book, so you have a useful paradigm to start imagining from.

Reflection Questions

- Why should you not reinvent the wheel?
- Should you focus on one thing or many?
- What are the pros and cons of jumping in on your own project?

Chapter 9: Learning Algorithms and Applications

"AI-assisted driving is a perfect platform for advancing fundamental human-centric artificial intelligence research while also producing practical applications." — ***Fei-Fei Li***

This chapter is going to largely focus on the current applications of machine learning and how it's being used at this very moment to solve very difficult processes. As you've already learned, machine learning - and especially neural networks and deep learning - have really opened doors for computers to be used to solve difficult problems that they perhaps wouldn't be able to so readily otherwise. The broadening of historical linear artificial intelligence, too, has opened the way for computers to be able not just to recognize patterns, but *abstract concepts*. This has been a major liberating force in artificial intelligence because it allows computers to do more than ever before with certain information.

Learning Algorithms

Before we get to anything else, let's start working with the idea of learning algorithms. We've already talked about a whole lot of different learning algorithms throughout this guidebook, but let's talk about what a learning algorithm is – conceptually, just so you know for future reference. A learning algorithm is anything that allows you to learn from data. These might be equations, or they might be software-based solutions for extracting useful data from a given data set. Either way, in the end, their goal is to give you some sort of data to work with and make predictions from in future cases.

In this capacity, we've already talked about a huge number of different learning algorithms in this book. However, learning algorithms are only the tip of the iceberg. As you go through the rest of the book and think about the applications of machine learning, try to really think about how the things that we've talked about *before* in this book could be used to actually implement these different things.

Text-based Services

The first thing that we're going to talk about in relation to machine learning applications is how machine learning has massively bolstered the ability of certain text-based services and allowed them to flourish. Specifically, we're going to be looking at web search and anti-spam.

Machine learning has massively benefited web search by combining various supervised and unsupervised learning techniques - like clustering, classification, and regression - to provide much better search results to the user. Sites that were previously only *okay* at indexing and ranking user search results were able to actively improve upon their algorithms and indexing ability by seeing *what users are most likely to click on after a search*, as well as *how likely they are to return to a search query after clicking on a page*. These allow computers to learn dynamically what a user is wanting when they enter a certain search term.

It also takes the time and activity levels into account. So, for example, if a lot of people started to click a certain link or news story around a certain time related to a certain celebrity, the algorithm would react quickly and learn in no time that something has *happened* regarding this celebrity. It would then adjust accordingly and start showing the more relevant news stories over less important information.

That's not the only way that machine learning has massively bolstered text-based services though. Another way is through the implementation of anti-spam algorithms. A lot of people tend to take this for granted, but the reason that your email inbox isn't absolutely cluttered with worthless junk is that computers have developed *very adept anti-spam algorithms*. The basis of these algorithms is simple: it rests in something called Bayes' theorem.

Bayes' theorem is a way of accurately calculating the probability of a given statement based not off *percentage-based probability,* but off *actual probability* concerning both false positives and false negatives. By applying this algorithm to incoming emails and weighing certain factors - such as whether the person has been corresponded with before, whether it *seems* like a spam email based off certain keywords, whether many of the same exact emails are being sent out, and so on - to determine dynamically and realistically whether a certain email is, indeed, a spam email, or if it's just a normal email that somebody is going to *really* want to receive.

These are only two examples of how machine learning is actively changing the world of computing as we know it. The landscape is massively shifting, and it's by and large thanks to this great technology.

Computer Vision

The implementation of computer-based vision is a tricky thing. How does one give a computer not only the ability to *see* but the ability to *process what they are seeing* and then *react accordingly*, much like humans do? That is a much more difficult question to answer.

The answer, though, lies again in machine learning - specifically deep learning and neural networks. There is a deep learning algorithm specifically tailored towards the emulation of animal retinae. To create this neural infrastructure, people would look at the neural networks of actual animal eyes and then use that to develop a model by which computers could develop a retina-like structure. This is only one example of the ways in which computers are slowly being given senses.

Some of the greatest examples of machine learning are in the combination of visual processing. One example could be the use of the iPhone X's front-facing camera to create a face recognition software that would only allow the proper user to gain access to the phone. This system can differentiate one face from another with extreme accuracy while also being able to tell *one particular user* regardless of their appearance. For example, somebody who normally doesn't wear makeup could still get into their phone when they had makeup on. Someone who normally doesn't wear glasses could still get into their phone when they started wearing them. These examples go on and on.

This is yet another example of how machine learning is being implemented to make smarter technology. This specific implementation is all about the use of deep learning and multiple neural networks which can detect most idiosyncrasies of a person's face - with enough precision that it's able to tell their face apart from any other given person's face. This is a major stride in terms of AI, and this is just one example.

Similar deep learning and machine learning algorithms have been used in the implementation of *augmented reality*, which uses the current field of vision within the camera to intelligently reflect some sort of computerized information to the user in a seamless manner. Machine learning technologies allow augmented reality software to tell one surface from another and have an "understanding" of the field of vision in the image.

Audio Processing

One of the most impressive applications of machine learning and deep learning is the implementation of various techniques to better process audio. Most people have smartphones nowadays that excellently display this tech right in the palm of your hand. If you have an Android or an iPhone, especially a newer model, chances are you've used this tech before.

Think back - when is the last time you used voice to type a text message, or you opened *Siri* or *Google Assistant* and asked it where something was or for restaurants near you? Machine learning is the powerful technique processing all this complex information.

Deep learning, again, is specifically the implementation engine of this. Older and more linear models would have hand-coded phrases, and the system would be able to tell if the user said one of these words or not. Modern models, instead, can break apart the parts of speech. They can detect breaks in speech to extrapolate where words start and end, and so forth, to figure out what is a sentence, a word, and the parts of speech, subject, and related phenomena are within the sentence.

Perhaps the most impressive example of this, aside from *Siri* and related digital assistants, is the automatic caption utility provided by things such as *YouTube*. In these systems, the audio of the video will be picked apart, and people who are speaking will have their speech analyzed, and captions will be created dynamically in accordance with the audio. While these systems didn't start out very good, as the machines have had time to learn and *Google*'s voice recognition in general has gotten better, (due at least partly to their work with translation and digital assistants and their heavy focus on the streamlining of everyday life through voice recognition), the general ability of the automatic captioning system to dynamically recognize and react to language has gotten much better. Even videos in that are not in English have fairly good voice recognition capabilities, with the abilities of the systems seeming to scale with the popularity of the language - backing up the notion that the systems have been improved through user experience as a natural extension of the machine learning paradigm.

Database Mining

Database mining is one of the most popular uses of machine learning since machine learning goes so naturally together with data analysis. Database mining is about drawing pertinent and important information from databases and then using that to train your machine. Data mining and machine learning are connected by the fact that machine learning is great at figuring out what information is *useful* in a dataset. This data can then be extracted and analyzed and kept for its own independent value.

This might be a tad confusing because technically you need to algorithmically train your software to start data mining in the first place. However, more conventional unsupervised methods are great at foregoing this and looking at a set of data as it is, then drawing the useful data from it through methods such as normalization and clustering. A solid algorithm for both dimensional reduction and clustering will allow you to effortlessly extract useful data from a data set, by going over it and determining what the most important data categories are.

Reflection Questions

- How has machine learning changed e-mail?
- Where does machine learning become useful in data analysis?
- In what ways has machine learning affected audio processing?

Chapter 10: Examples of Successful Machine Learning

*"There is huge demand for artificial intelligence technologies." — **Yuri Milner***

In this chapter, we're going to be looking at *outcomes*. With the context of the world of machine learning, what are the altogether most successful examples of machine learning? Some of this is going to be rehashing some of the things that we've already discussed, and others will regard working with new concepts that we haven't discussed in depth. By the end of this chapter, you're going to have a firm grasp on the overall potential of machine learning models by understanding how they've already been used.

Spotify and Pandora

Spotify and *Pandora* serve as some of the most successful examples of innocuous machine learning. Though it's not very *in your face*, it is still a fundamental part of the experience of using these services, especially *Pandora*. Machine learning is used in gaining an understanding of what a person likes or dislikes regarding music. Music is categorized as having many different traits upon being entered into the system (or, in *Spotify*'s case, through user-based learning.)

There are two mechanisms by which these can recommend new music to you. The model that *Pandora* uses is heavily based off analysis of the music itself. Songs are analyzed as having certain qualities that make it up. A user who likes a song likes these qualities, obviously. In using the *Pandora* application, people will like or dislike songs that they have a particular feeling toward.

The qualities of these songs are then compared against each other to better tailor the individual's musical tastes.

For example, two sadder songs that are both in a minor key and are upbeat may be liked by the user. If, then, a sadder song that is *not* upbeat is played, and the user dislikes it, the system may conclude that the user likes songs that are in a minor key and that are upbeat. As a result, the system will adapt and thus play the user sadder, faster songs. This continued learning experience allows the system to dynamically interpret how a user may feel about certain music.

The other model is the user-based model. This one is used a bit by *Pandora* but far more expansively by *Spotify*. In this model, you simply analyze what different types of music go along with certain artists that people listen to. There is a good chance that other people will follow similar patterns. In this case, it's just recognition of the fact that there are patterns and characteristic commonalities between music.

This can lead to some pretty neat results, too. All this data and machine learning are used by *Spotify* to cluster music together according to people's interests. In this, *Spotify* has created some cool genres that previously wouldn't have existed. These are, for example, *shiver pop* and *gauze pop*, clusters which were recognized by *Spotify* and needed a distinct name. When you analyze the relationships that exist within music, and that connect the songs that people listen to, you start to come to conclusions about genre delineations, and that's actually a very cool and unexpected outcome of machine learning.

PayPal

This is perhaps one of the most practical things in this book: fraud detection. We haven't really talked about fraud detection at length, but it's one of the coolest and most practical uses of machine learning that has yet come forward. It's normal for financial institutions and the like to need some mechanism by which they're able to determine whether fraud has occurred or might occur.

Older methods required that either people evaluated fraud by hand, or very rigid methodologies like linear functions were used. Modern technology and neural networking, in particular, have given us the ability to look at all of this in a far more abstract way. For example, we can now look at the actual behaviors of the user and what they're doing. These allow *PayPal* to determine these behaviors in a fluid way and understand not just fraud, but the behavior that goes *into* fraud. This allows them to prevent it in the future, as well as recognize it with more immediacy than the old models would have allowed by noticing behaviors before they become a major issue.

Uber

Uber is yet another example of a tech giant that is using machine learning to their advantage. And, indeed, Uber benefits massively from their implementations of machine learning technology. It could be argued that the service as a whole completely *depends upon* machine learning in its day to day interactions.

Machine learning is used by Uber to determine information about things such as when a person can expect to be picked up, as well as when drivers are most likely to arrive. This is a natural result because Uber wants the information it displays to its user to be as accurate as possible so that they get an incredible service experience.

As a result, whenever you use Uber, the service will review an absolutely massive number of trips that have *already happened,* and then extrapolate information from those trips to apply them to the trip that *you* booked. This information is a boon for Uber.

Facebook

You've probably already noticed how Facebook uses machine learning all of the time. There are a huge number of applications that utilize artificial intelligence on *Facebook*. When was the last time that you were tagged in a picture? When was the last time you went to tag somebody in a picture?

Maybe it's been a moment. However, if you've used this feature any time recently, then you're aware of how eerily accurate *Facebook*'s facial recognition software has become. It can allow you to tag people who perhaps you've not even added. It's seriously good.

How good? Well, it can detect a human face within a quarter of one percent of a human's accuracy. No, not a quarter of a human's accuracy. A quarter of *one percent*. These algorithms are nearly up to the level of the raw ability of humans themselves to determine who is who and differentiate one person from another.

This is not the only way that *Facebook* utilizes machine learning. Even its search results heavily use different machine algorithms to determine who you may know and who you may want to add. This is intended to make it easier to have a more productive search than you might otherwise. The end result is that you start to feel like when you look something up on *Facebook*, you will have a good chance of finding whatever it is you're looking for.

Facebook has come under some scrutiny due to the raw amount of data that it has accumulated from its users, as well as the various manners in which they've treated this data. Nonetheless, the strides made by *Facebook* have been tremendous. *Facebook* also uses a huge amount of machine learning in its promoted posts feature to target posts that take advantage of the promoted posts feature at the people who are most likely to *benefit* from the post itself. It will target the posts to geographical areas, and different interest clusters that they feel are most likely to enjoy the content of the post.

Speaking of interest clusters, *Facebook* also has a highly sophisticated advertising algorithm that specializes in aiming advertisements at the users who are most likely to click on said advertisements. You can see for yourself some of the different ways in which *Facebook* categorizes you is by going to your privacy settings on your profile and looking under the Ads tab. Here, you'll see the different interest clusters that *Facebook* has placed you in based on the posts that you've made on your *Facebook* as well as the pages that you've liked on *Facebook*.

With one of the highest market caps of any social media company in the world - if not the absolute highest - *Facebook* serves as a constant reminder of how smart technology can massively bolster a company and make a lot of money in the process.

In a world where technology is the catalyst to all else, data - and the proper usage of that data - is king.

Gmail

Gmail is yet another of *Google* outdoing themselves in terms of machine learning. In this implementation, *Google* uses its immense collection of data and linguistic capabilities to determine the content of a given email and then give the user three possible messages to choose from as a Smart Reply.

If you use *Gmail* often, you've probably already been surprised about how good this technology is at guessing what the email that you've been sent said and giving you an appropriate set of smart responses to it. Even if you don't use them very often, they still are an extremely cool example of machine learning in action.

Gmail is a great example of machine learning for yet another reason - they have one of the best spam filters of any popular email service on the internet. There are few email services that are so good at what they do as *Google*. *Gmail* offers a plethora of different services, and not the least of which is their extremely sophisticated spam filter. Using a combination of different algorithms, *Google* has created a system that will allow you to use your email account for years without ever getting a spam message in your email inbox. At least, without one signing up for a given service. Anecdotally, in all the time that I've had a *Gmail* account, only one email has leaked into my primary inbox.

While there are a number of different email providers with very in-depth spam filters, the sheer sophistication of *Google*'s makes it incredibly worthy to note. However, if you were looking for a successful implementation of machine learning, you can't go wrong with looking at all of the spam filters in general.

Closing

With that, we've discussed a number of different applications of machine learning and how you can see this amazing technology in action. It's used for everything from recommender systems like those of *Spotify, Pandora*, and *Netflix,* all the way to dynamic language translation and then for spam email detection and to fraud detection. You can see already how machine learning is having an incredibly huge impact on the world and taking it by storm one application at a time. In the following chapter, we're going to be taking a look at what you can expect of machine learning in the future.

Reflection Questions

- How does PayPal benefit from using machine learning?
- What are some of the ways that Google uses machine learning?
- What type of distance algorithm does Uber most likely use?

Chapter 11:
Future of Machine Learning

"I deeply believe that any business that doesn't make an investment in machine learning in 2017 will fall behind their competition." – ***Mansour Raad***

One of the hardest things to predict is the future, especially when it comes to technology. Perhaps the best-known example of predictable computing is the classic *Moore's Law*, which states that every two years, the number of transistors on an integrated circuit would double. However, even time has proven this wrong, as diminishing returns in correspondence to the actual productivity of greater numbers of transistors would decrease, and as it began to become more and more difficult to create worthwhile materials at that small of a level.

So, what does this show us as budding computer and data scientists? That technology can be hard to predict - especially when it's so nebulous and open-ended as is machine learning. However, machine learning has as bright of a future as anything else related to computer science and artificial intelligence - that is to say, *very* bright.

So, what can one expect from the broad field of machine learning in the years to come? To be honest, a whole lot. Let's look at this by individual industry.

Finance

The finance industry will be one of the major benefactors of machine learning as it becomes more and more sophisticated. The tricky part of it all is that finance is in some ways unpredictable. However, people tend to underrate how much patterns can play into the actual timeline of the finance industry.

For example, the crash of 2008 was predicted by the people who shorted the housing market by recognizing patterns from prior economic crashes, as well as the current state of subprime mortgages in the industry. A machine geared towards recognizing patterns could make investors aware of these sorts of things before they happen - and potentially give them the means to profit off it if they're unscrupulous.

In some manners, though, finance *is* unpredictable. The stock market on average tends to follow some patterns. Systems that can learn these idiosyncrasies of the stock market and then adapt and recognize different features in the same way that we can recognize facial features - implying, of course, neural networks - can be a massive boon to the finance industry. This is because it will allow the progression beyond strictly linear models of economic prediction. This means more responsive models and better predictive algorithms.

Language

One can expect families worldwide to flourish as well as international business to benefit massively as the linguistic capabilities of artificial intelligence grow stronger. Technology will develop such that it will be able to process speech instantaneously from strangers. If both people were to wear this headset, this would mean that two people - regardless of what language they spoke - would be able to understand each other perfectly. In essence, the creation of a real-life Babelfish - again, so long as the technology was there.

But let's say for a moment that this technology doesn't come to exist. One way or another, the implications for machine learning on machine translation are massive. We talked earlier in the book about how the linear nature of technology was going to change in response to the development of more advanced machine learning concepts, such as neural networks that are far more intricate and responsive than traditional linear methodologies.

Upon becoming advanced enough, for instance, the transcription and subtitling industries may change massively in response to the fact that computers are now better able to understand what people are saying. Computers may be able to far more accurately predict what people are saying and react in response to this, making it possible for computers to do entire subtitle tracks and transcripts and only have a human there for the editing and review process - which may not even be necessary once the technology becomes advanced enough.

Medical Industry

Machine learning is also finding a use in the medical industry as we start to look toward the capabilities of machine learning for the medical and pharmaceutical industries. It's already possible to use deep learning as a means of predicting drug interactions and drug outcomes. It's also possible to use deep learning as a means of predicting chemical interactions between different substances.

This is going to have a major impact on the future as computers become more advanced and the algorithms powering them do as well. We're going to see the medical and pharmaceutical industries save a lot of time as they start using technology to model possible interactions and see how they could go. This will also save a lot of money that is otherwise coming out for research budgets.

Self-Driving Cars

This is already slowly becoming a reality thanks to the contributions of companies such as Tesla, Toyota, and Honda. Self-driving cars are the most obvious application of machine learning to our everyday lives, but they don't quite get enough credit for how much of an impact they're going to have on our future directly.

There will be a world where you can just get in your car and start going somewhere by putting in the name of the location on your GPS and letting the car do the rest. You can kick back and relax while your car does all the heavy lifting for you. Already, we are working on making the decision-making process of a car as complex as possible and trying to allot for as many possibilities as we can. There are complex moral and philosophical *no-win* situations that are even having data gathered for them thanks to projects created by people such as researchers at MIT. These are going to be directly used for the development of advanced intelligence in cars.

The autopilot mode in cars has gotten some bad press as of late as Tesla cars have had a few hiccups. However, the current state of the technology says very little about the future state of the technology. The implementation of self-driving cars is but one way that we're going to see machine learning start to have a massive impact on our everyday lives.

Robots and Androids

This is perhaps one of the most hotly debated topics in all of machine learning and deep learning specifically. Many people don't have any desire for robots to take on a humanoid form; others see it as inevitable, and potentially the only course for society to take. Indeed, it would be somewhat neat to have humanoid robots that would do our bidding or, at the very least, take care of many of the tasks that we don't want to do ourselves.

This is a long way off, though. However, with that said, we are slowly gaining stronger and stronger technological capabilities. For example, Turing complete chatbots already exist which do a fantastic job of mimicking human emotion and responding appropriately, making it seem as though a real person is on the other line.

In addition, developments in computer vision, as we've already discussed, would allow the technology to be used in a massively beneficial way. For example, a robot or android assistant could recognize things around the house and react accordingly. They could, for example, be able to pick up your clothes and put them away for you or be programmed to make meals for you.

This sort of projected humanoid is a long way off - but is it potentially closer than we give it credit for? After all, many of the features already exist, though in imperfect forms. For example, being able to recognize and react to speech in an appropriate way. These robots could perhaps even speak every known language if their translation faculties were good enough. Computer vision and image recognition are getting better, as well. We are, in effect, programming each component one by one and slowly implementing them. So, this future is perhaps not so distant. We have all the pieces. Maybe it's just about cutting them correctly and then putting them all together.

Closing

So, really, what did we learn about the future possibilities of machine learning? We learned that anything we can imagine, machine learning pretty much is capable of doing. At this point, it's just about finding those things that we dream about being able to do and then actually implementing the code to *do* them.

Reflection Questions

- How can one expect machine learning to benefit finance?
- Are humanoid robots a realistic goal of machine learning? Why or why not?
- How will the medical industry benefit from machine learning?

Conclusion

With that, we've made it to the end of this book. It's been quite the ride, thank you for sticking it out with me. In closing, I would like to make a few more comments and give you some direction going forward.

First, I've already discussed the best practices of machine learning. I'd just like to drive those home again. You really need to be applying yourself and trying out some new projects. It's through this that you're going to start to grow as a programmer. More than that, there are some really incredible things happening with machine learning as we speak, and a good number of them are happening in the open source communities. (You can thank the fact that nerds love both robots and open-source software.)

So, you should most definitely take advantage of that. There are projects all over *Github* and on sites like *Reddit* where you can start dipping your toes into the world of machine learning.

Also, there is a whole lot of information out there about artificial intelligence, because let's be honest - it's super cool. Toy around with the numerous free textbooks that are available for machine learning and find your own specific niche that you want to work within, then spend a while doing projects within that niche. If you do that, you're going to find yourself slowly becoming a more and more accomplished person in general - both as a programmer, and as a specialist in your niche. When I was just getting into natural language processing, I started learning from a free textbook that was available online. There is a wealth of resources available to the initiated who want to learn about it.

Speaking of *Reddit*, by the way, another thing that I would highly encourage you to do is get involved with machine learning communities. Yes, those exist, and they're quite active. People who like machine learning tend, believe it or not, to *really* like machine learning. It makes sense, partially because of all the potential that rests in the technology, coupled with the fact that it's such an intense field of study, starting to get good with machine learning involves devoting quite a large part of yourself to the study.

There are a number of communities that are easy to find just by searching around on the internet. These are an extremely valuable resource because it will ensure that you have friends who share the same interests as you. However, it's also a valuable resource because it gives you an opportunity to bounce information out there and get feedback on it. Having a feedback loop as a programmer is essentially the computer science equivalent of peer review. People being able to tell you what you're doing wrong and could be doing better is incredibly important to somebody who is trying to get into a new niche.

There is an extremely long road ahead. Machine learning is a fickle and complicated science, and you've got the benefit of joining into a sensation that is absolutely changing the world while it's also a relatively young technology and not completely saturated. However, the flip side of this is that sometimes you're going to get completely stumped. The things that you're working with are incredibly difficult. Working with algorithms is not easy. Working with the advanced mathematics isn't easy either. What's especially not easy is working with all of this in tandem with something you may or may not know a lot about, like data analysis or finance or linguistics. However, if you keep going with it, I guarantee that you're going to reap a lot of rewards just by virtue of your dedication to such a young science.

In essence, keep your head about you. Try not to pull your hair out. Join communities of other machine learning nerds and try to ask them questions when the mood or occasion strikes. More than anything, keep trying and keep your head up. I hope that I've helped you in your mission of understanding machine learning and machine learning algorithms. Good luck!

About the Author

Steven Cooper is a data scientist and worked as a software engineer at multiple startups. Now he works as a freelancer and helping big companies in their marketing and statistical analysis using machine learning and deep learning techniques.

Steven has many years of experience with coding in Python and has given several seminars on the practical applications of data science, machine learning, and deep learning over the years. In addition he delivers training and coaching services that help technical professionals advance their careers.

He loves to write and talk about data science, machine learning, and Python, and he is very motivated to help people developing data-driven solutions without necessarily requiring a machine learning background.

When not writing or programming, Steven enjoys spending time with his daughters or relaxing at the lake with his wife.

www.ingramcontent.com/pod-product-compliance
Lightning Source LLC
La Vergne TN
LVHW091420190726
843491LV00006B/1525

9783903331174